# The wonder of fathers

# C. R. Gibson®

## FINE GIFTS SINCE 1870

*All images © Hulton Getty Picture Collection.*
*Picture research by Jon Wright.*
*Design by Keith Jackson.*
*All text, unless otherwise attributed, by Jonathan Bicknell.*

*Developed by Publishing Services Corporation, Nashville, Tennessee.*

*Published by C. R. Gibson®*
*C. R. Gibson® is a registered trademark of Thomas Nelson, Inc.*
*Nashville, Tennessee 37214*
*Printed and bound by L. Rex Printing Company Limited, China*

*ISBN 0-7667-6755-8*
*UPC 0-82272-46685-2*
*GB4152*

# The wonder of fathers

"To follow in your footsteps was all I ever wanted."

"It is a **wise father** who **knows** his own **child**"

– William Shakespeare

"Children.
One is one,
two is fun,
three is a
houseful."

– American Proverb

"Well, it just doesn't get any better than this."

"Honor
thy father...
for this is the first
commandment
that comes
with a promise."

"Home is where
the heart is."

"As they say:
like
father,
like son."

17

"To see the **pride** in your **eyes** was good **enough** for me."

"But even when
I failed,
I was still good
enough for
you."

"I just couldn't wait for you to come home."

"You helped me
feel big
even when I
was little."

24

"And showed me **how** to care for the things **you** care for."

"To me you were always
the best."

"Your arms never **failed** to catch and hold me **tight.**"

"For **you** will always be, the one to whom my **first**  words were, 'Daddy, Daddy, Daddy.'"